MULTIPLE-CHOICE
ENGLISH
Practice Test 10

Guidance for completing this Test.

1. Read the passages carefully.

2. Read the questions thoroughly.

3. Read the answers carefully.

4. Choose what you think is the correct answer carefully.

5. Underline or circle the answer, immediately after the question.

6. Transfer the LETTER **A,B,C,D,E** or **N** to the answer sheet.

7. Make sure to mark the answer box like [—] not [✓].

8. Check carefully that you have transferred your correct answer.

9. This test lasts for **50 minutes.**

PUPIL'S NAME _____

TOTAL MARK (Out of 60)	

Read this passage and answer the questions which follow. If there are any words you don't understand you may find them in the Glossary at the end of the test.

SANTA'S DAEMONS

1.　　　　It was well known that no harm can come to Santa Claus while he is in the Laughing Valley, for the fairies, and ryls, and knooks all protect him. But on Christmas Eve he drives his reindeer out into the big world, carrying a sleigh load of toys and
5.　　pretty gifts to the children; and this was the time and the occasion when his enemies had the best chance to injure him. So the Daemons laid their plans and awaited the arrival of Christmas Eve.

　　　　The moon shone big and white in the sky, and the snow lay crisp and sparkling on the ground as Santa Claus cracked his
10.　　whip and sped away out of the Valley into the great world beyond. The roomy sleigh was packed full with huge sacks of toys, and as the reindeer dashed onward our jolly old Santa laughed and whistled and sang with joy. For in all his merry life this was the one day in the year when he was happiest--the day he lovingly
15.　　bestowed the treasures of his workshop upon the little children.

　　　　It would be a busy night for him, he well knew. As he whistled and shouted and cracked his whip again, he reviewed in mind all the towns and cities and farmhouses where he was expected, and figured that he had just enough presents to go
20.　　around and make every child happy. The reindeer knew exactly what was expected of them, and dashed along so swiftly that their feet scarcely seemed to touch the snow-covered ground.

　　　　Suddenly a strange thing happened: a rope shot through the moonlight and a big noose that was on the end of it settled over the
25.　　arms and body of Santa Claus and drew tight. Before he could resist or even cry out he was jerked from the seat of the sleigh and tumbled head foremost into a snowbank, while the reindeer rushed onward with the load of toys and carried it quickly out of sight and sound.

30.　　　　Such a surprising experience confused old Santa for a moment, and when he had collected his senses he found that the wicked Daemons had pulled him from the snowdrift and bound him tightly with many coils of the stout rope. And then they carried the kidnapped Santa Claus away to their mountain, where
35.　　they thrust the prisoner into a secret cave and chained him to the rocky wall so that he could not escape.

　　　　"Ha, ha!" laughed the Daemons, rubbing their hands together with cruel glee. "What will the children do now? How they will cry

40. and scold and storm when they find there are no toys in their stockings and no gifts on their Christmas trees! And what a lot of punishment they will receive from their parents, and how they will flock to our Caves of Selfishness, and Envy, and Hatred, and Malice! We have done a mighty clever thing, we Daemons of the Caves!"

Answer the following questions. Look back over the passage. You should choose the _best_ answer and mark its letter on your answer sheet.

1. When was the most dangerous time for Santa Claus ?

A.   ...living in his home territory of Laughing Valley.
B.   ...climbing down chimneys to deliver toys.
C.   ...tending to the reindeer in their forests.
D.   ...moving out into the big world from Laughing Valley.
E.   ...making the toys in his workshop.

2. What was used to jerk Santa Claus out of his seat ?

A.   ...two of the reindeers   B.   ...the fairies and ryls
C.   ...the roomy sleigh   D.   ...the neighbouring knooks
E.   ...a noose made from a rope

3. On the happiest day of the year Santa

A.   ...fed his reindeer and counted the toys.
B.   ...gave a party for the fairies, ryls and knooks.
C.   ...gave out the products of his workshop.
D.   ...prepared the sleigh for his journeys.
E.   ...drives the sleigh across the clouds.

4. Santa Claus was captured by the

A.   ...Daemons   B.   ...Knooks   C.   ...Fairies
D.   ...Ryls   E.   ...Reindeer

5. How many caves will the parents have to visit ?

A.   One   B.   Two   C.   Three
D.   Four   E.   Five

2.

6. How was Santa Claus kept imprisoned ?

A. He was locked up in his workshop.
B. He fell into a snowbank and couldn't get out.
C. He was tied up in farmhouses in the cities.
D. He was tied with rope and chained to a wall.
E. He was blindfolded with hands and feet bound.

7. The night of Christmas Eve was

A. dark, cloudy and raining.
B. bright with sparkling crisp snow.
C. bright, dismal and frightening.
D. stormy, moonless and ghostly.
E. exciting, expectant and busy.

8. The Daemons were rubbing their hands with cruel glee because

A. they had captured the reindeer.
B. they were opening their toys and presents.
C. they weren't getting any toys or presents.
D. they were having a party for Santa Claus.
E. the children wouldn't have any presents or toys.

9. What happened the reindeer when Santa was captured ?

A. ...the fairies rescued them.
B. ...they carried on with their load of toys.
C. ...the Daemons captured them as well.
D. ...the parents saved them.
E. ...they went back to the Laughing Valley.

10. Santa's homeland, Laughing Valley, was given this name

A. because the fairies and knooks were comedians.
B. when the reindeers laughed at Santa learning to ski.
C. after the toy, the Laughing Monkeys.
D. when the Daemons left the valley to go to the caves.
E. because of the happiness and joy of providing toys for children.

The following passage contains a number of mistakes. You have to find the mistakes. On each line there is either _one_ mistake or _no_ mistake. Find the group of words in which there is a mistake and mark the letter for it on your answer sheet. If there is no mistake, mark N.

First, look for the _spelling_ mistakes.

11. Now it so / hapened that on / this Christmas / Eve the good
    A   B   C   D   N

12. Santa Claus had / taken with him / in his slay / Nuter the Ryl,
    A   B   C   D   N

13. Peter the Knook, / Kilter the Pixie, / and a small / fairy named
    A   B   C   D   N

14. Wisk, his four / favourite assistants. / These little / people he had
    A   B   C   D   N

15. often found / very useful in / helped him / to distribute
    A   B   C   D   N

16. his gifts to the / children, and / when there / master was so
    A   B   C   D   N

17. suddenly dragged / from the / sleigh they / where all snugly
    A   B   C   D   N

18. tuked underneath / the seat, / where the / sharp wind
    A   B   C   D   N

19. could not reach / them and / make them cold. / The tiny
    A   B   C   D   N

20. immortals new / nothing of / the capture / of Santa Claus
    A   B   C   D   N

until some time after he had disappeared.

Now look for _punctuation_ mistakes.

But finally they

21. missed his / cheery voice, / and as thei'r / master always
    A   B   C   D   N

4.

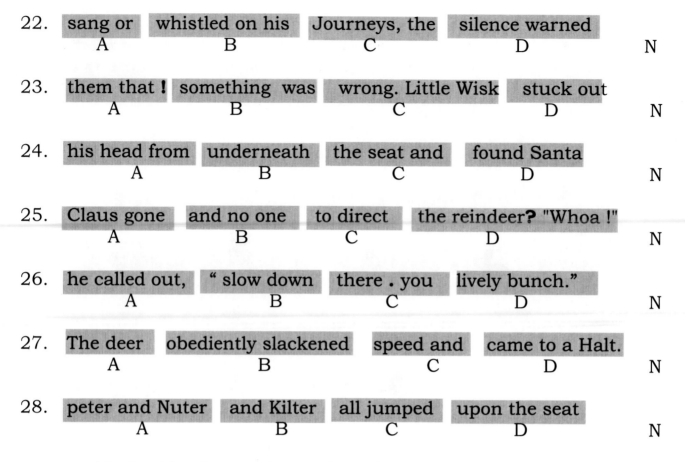

22. sang or | whistled on his | Journeys, the | silence warned | N
    A | B | C | D

23. them that **!** | something was | wrong. Little Wisk | stuck out | N
    A | B | C | D

24. his head from | underneath | the seat and | found Santa | N
    A | B | C | D

25. Claus gone | and no one | to direct | the reindeer? "Whoa !" | N
    A | B | C | D

26. he called out, | " slow down | there . you | lively bunch." | N
    A | B | C | D

27. The deer | obediently slackened | speed and | came to a Halt. | N
    A | B | C | D

28. peter and Nuter | and Kilter | all jumped | upon the seat | N
    A | B | C | D

and looked back over the track made by the sleigh.

**Read this passage and answer the questions which follow.
If there are any words you don't understand you may find
them in the Glossary at the end of the test.**

PENNILESS BY LETTER

1.   Then Dr. Sampson wheeled round in his office chair.
"I have a letter for you from your guardian, Rodney," he said. "Here
it is. Do me the favour to read it here."
With some wonder Rodney took the letter and read as follows:

5.   DEAR RODNEY--
              I have bad news to communicate. As you know,
I was left by your father in charge of you and your fortune. I have
never told you the amount, but I will say now that it was about
fifty thousand dollars. Until two years ago I kept it intact but
10   then began a series of reverses in which my own fortune was
swallowed up. In the hope of relieving myself I regret to say
that I was tempted to use your money. That went also, and
now of the whole sum there remains two hundred and fifty dollars,
enough to pay the balance of your school bills, leaving you
15. penniless.

How much I regret this I cannot tell you. I shall leave New York at once. I do not care at present to say where I shall go, but I shall try to make good the loss, and eventually restore to you your lost fortune. I may be successful or I may not. I shall do my best

20. and I hope in time to have better news to communicate.

One thing I am glad to say. I have a casket containing your mother's jewels. These are intact. I shall send you the casket by express, knowing that you will wish to keep them out of regard for your mother's memory. In case you are reduced to the

25. necessity of pawning or selling them, I am sure that your mother, could she be consulted, would advise you to do so. This would be better than to have you suffer from want.

There is nothing further for me to write except to repeat my regret, and renew my promise to make up your lost fortune if

30. I shall ever to able to do so.

Your Guardian,
BENJAMIN FIELDING.

Rodney read this like one dazed. In an instant he was reduced from the position of a favourite of fortune to a needy boy,

35. with his living to make. He could not help recalling what had passed between his friend David and himself earlier in the day. Now he was as poor as David--poorer, in fact for David had a chance to learn a trade that would yield him a living, while he was utterly without resources, except in having an unusually good education.

40. "Well," said Dr. Sampson, "have you read your letter?"
"Yes, sir. Here is my letter, doctor. You can read it for yourself."
Dr. Sampson's face changed as he read Rodney's letter. It changed and hardened, and his expression became quite different from that to which Rodney had been accustomed.

45. "This is a bad business, Rodney," said the doctor in a hard tone, "since that was a handsome fortune which your father left you."
"Yes, sir. I never knew before how much it amounted to," Rodney announced in a surprised voice.
"You only learn when you have lost it. Mr. Fielding has treated you

50. shamefully," the Doctor continued in a reassuring manner.

29. Who wrote the letter to Rodney ?

A. Dr. Sampson
C. Rodney's guardian
E. Rodney's teacher
B. Rodney's mother
D. Rodney's father

30. The first thing that the letter states is

A. Dr. Sampson turned in his office chair.
B. Dr. Sampson asks Rodney to read the letter.
C. Dr. Sampson told Rodney he had a letter for him.
D. The letter states that there is bad news.
E. Rodney is told that he has a fortune.

31. From where is Rodney's guardian leaving ?

A. ...his place of work   B. ...New York
C. ...Dr. Sampson's office   D. ...Rodney's house
E. ...Rodney's school

32. Rodney's guardian has lost Rodney his fortune which was

A. 50,000 dollars   B. 50,000 pounds
C. 250 pounds   D. 250 dollars
E. a casket of jewels

33. How did Dr. Sampson react when he read Rodney's letter ?

A. ...he was angry with Rodney.
B. ...he wasn't surprised.
C. ...his face and his tone hardened.
D. ...he was delighted that Rodney still had the jewels.
E. ...he said that he would take the information to the police.

34. How was Rodney going to get his mother's jewels ?

A. He had to go and collect them.
B. They were to be delivered to his school.
C. His guardian would deliver them to Dr. Sampson.
D. They were to be sent to Rodney by express.
E. His guardian would deliver them personally.

35. Rodney's guardian lost the fortune because

A. it had been stolen.   B. he gave it to the poor.
C. he lent it to a friend.   D. he spent the money.
E. he gambled it on horses.

7.

36. The lines that convey the bit of good news in the letter are

A.   lines 11 and 12   B.   lines 14 and 15
C.   lines 17 and 18   D.   lines 21 and 22
E.   lines 29 and 30

37. In which way did the letter affect Rodney's relationship
    with his friend, David ?

A.   Rodney would now be richer than David.
B.   David would now be poorer than Rodney.
C.   Rodney would now be poorer than David.
D.   Rodney and David would both be rich.
E.   Rodney and David would no longer be friends.

38. The advice that Benjamin Fielding gave Rodney
    about the jewels was

A.   ...keep them in memory of his mother.
B.   ...give them to a charity of his choice.
C.   ...that he, Benjamin Fielding, would keep them.
D.   ...to consult his mother about what to do.
E.   ...to pawn or sell the jewels rather than suffer from want.

39. The best meaning of the word **communicate** in **line 20** is

A.   ...to travel abroad   B.   ...to meet regularly
C.   ...to make known   D.   ...to meditate
E.   ...to make friends

40. The phrase meaning **"owning absolutely nothing "** is in

A.   lines 6 and 7   B.   lines 13 and 14
C.   lines 38 and 39   D.   lines 17 and 18
E.   lines 45 and 46

41. The Adverbs in **lines 18 and 50** are

A.   restore and learn   B.   eventually and shamefully
C.   loss and continued   D.   make and reassuring
E.   shall and manner

8.

42. What punctuation is in both **line 3** and **line 41** ?

A. exclamation marks   B. semi-colons
C. question marks   D. speech marks
E. commas

**Read this passage and answer the questions which follow.
If there are any words you don't understand you may find
them in the Glossary at the end of the test.**

BARKING BABOON

1.   In the days when everybody started fair, Best Beloved, the
Leopard lived in a place called the High Veldt. Remember it wasn't
the Low Veldt, or the Bush Veldt, or the Sour Veldt, but the
exclusively bare, hot shiny High Veldt, where there was sand and
5.   sandy-coloured rock and tufts of exclusively sandy-yellowish grass.
The Giraffe and the Zebra and the Eland and the Koodoo
and the Hartebeest lived there: and they were exclusively sandy-
yellow-brownish all over; but the Leopard, he was the most exclusive
sandiest-yellowest-brownest of them all -- a greyish-yellowish
10. catty-shaped kind of beast, and he matched the exclusively
yellowish-greyish-brownish colour of the High Veldt to one hair.
This was very bad for the Giraffe and the Zebra and the rest of
them: for he would lie down by an exclusively yellowish-greyish
brownish stone or clump of grass, and when the Giraffe or the Zebra
15. or the Eland or the Koodoo or the Bush-Buck or the Bonte-Buck
came by he would surprise them out of their intimidating lives.
He would indeed !
      And, also, there was an Ethiopian with bows and
arrows (an exclusively greyish-brownish-yellowish man he was
20. then), who lived on the High Veldt with the Leopard: and the two
used to hunt together -- the Ethiopian with his bows and arrows,
and the Leopard exclusively with his teeth and claws -- till the
Giraffe and the Eland and the Koodoo and the Quagga and all the
rest of them didn't know which way to escape from Best Beloved.
25. They didn't indeed!
      After a long time -- things lived for ever so long in those
days -- they learned to avoid anything that looked like a Leopard
or an Ethiopian: and bit by bit -- the Giraffe began it, because his
legs were the longest -- they went away from the High Veldt.
30. They scuttled for days and days till they came to a great forest,
exclusively full of trees and bushes and stripy, speckly, patchy-
blotchy shadows, and there they hid.

9.

35. After another long time, what with standing half in the shade and half out of it, and what with the slippery slidy shadows of the trees falling on them, the Giraffe grew blotchy, and the Zebra grew stripy, and the Eland and the Koodoo grew darker, with little wavy grey lines on their backs like bark on a tree-trunk.

40. Though you could hear and smell these two, you could very seldom see them, and then only when you knew precisely where to look. They had a beautiful time in the exclusively speckly-spickly shadows of the forest, while the Leopard and the Ethiopian ran about the exclusively greyish-yellowish-reddish High Veldt outside, wondering where all their breakfasts and their dinners and their teas had gone. At last they were so hungry that they ate

45. rats and beetles and rock-rabbits, the Leopard and the Ethiopian, and then they had the Big Tummy-ache, both together: and then they met Baviaan -- the dog-headed, barking Baboon, who is Quite the Wisest Animal in All South Africa.

43. The animal which is the wisest in all South africa is

A.   ...the Leopard   B.   ...the Giraffe
C.   ...the Koodoo   D.   ...the Zebra
E.   ...the Baboon

44. The Ethiopian hunted with

A.   ...spears and machetes   B.   ...bows and arrows
C.   ...teeth and claws   D.   ...guns and nets
E.   ...traps and snares

45. The name of the most famous leopard is

A.   Baviaan   B.   Big Tummy   C.   Best Beloved
D.   Ethiopian   E.   Quagga

46. Where did the leopard live ?

A.   Ethiopia   B.   Sour Veldt   C.   Low Veldt
D.   Bush Veldt   E.   High Veldt

47. The word which is used most times in **paragraph 1** is

A. Leopard   B. Veldt   C. exclusively
D. yellowest   E. High

48. The two animals which were rarely seen in the last paragraph were

A. the rock-rabbit and the rats   B. the baboon and the Leopard
C. the Eland and the Koodoo   D. the Giraffe and the Zebra
E. the beetles and the dog

49. How did the animals on the High Veldt try to escape from the hunting Ethiopian and the Leopard ?

A. ...they travelled down to the river bank.
B. ...they lay down in the sand and grass.
C. ...they moved to higher ground.
D. ...they moved to a great forest full of trees.
E. ...they changed their colour to blend in with their surroundings.

50. Which animal started the movement of the animals away from the High Veldt ?

A. the Giraffe   B. the Zebra   C. the Leopard
D. the Quagga   E. the Hartebeest

51. What effect did eating rats and beetles and rock-rabbits have on the Leopard and the Ethiopian ?

A. ...they starved to death.   B. ...they ran out of food.
C. ...they became sick.   D. ...they stopped eating.
E. ...they started to eat plants.

52. The Giraffe was the first animal to leave the High Veldt because

A. ...it had more spots than the Leopard.
B. ...it had the longest neck.
C. ...it knew how to get to the great forest.
D. ...it was the wisest animal.
E. ...it had the longest legs.

11.

53. The word **" exclusively "** is used repeatedly in the passage. It means

A. ...completely   B. ...excellently   C. ...rarely
D. ...dramatically   E. ...conveniently

54. The words **dog-headed** and **barking** in **line 47** are

A. nouns   B. pronouns   C. verbs
D. adjectives   E. adverbs

55. The words **Best Beloved**, **South Africa** and **Baviaan** have capital letters because they are

A. Compound words   B. Hyphenated words
C. Collective Nouns   D. Comparative adjectives
E. Proper nouns

General Section
To answer these questions, you may have to think about the passages you have read. Look back at these if you need to. Look also at the Index and Glossary.

56. (a)   Apostrophes are used

A. ...to identify proper nouns.   B. ...to indicate a question.
C. ...to show abbreviations.   D. ...to complete a sentence.

(b).   The part of the Test which has **no** names of animals is

A. SANTA'S DAEMONS   B. PENNILESS BY LETTER
C. BARKING BABOON   D. General Section

57. (a)   Another word for a story is

A. sentence   B. paragraph
C. essay   D. poem

12.

(b). The sentence which has a grammatical error is

A. With a crash the thieves broke the jeweller's window.
B. We were not allowed to touch the food.
C. John ridden the bicycle down the street.
D. The injured climber had fallen from a high rock.

58. (a) What **"part of speech"** could be described as words which add information about nouns and pronouns ?

A. adverbs   B. verbs
C. compound words   D. adjectives

(b). The Contents page of a book is placed

A. ...at the end of the book.   B. ...at the beginning of the book.
C. ...on the outside of the book.   D. ...in the middle of the book.

59. (a) The adjectives in the GLOSSARY are

A. bound / bestowed   B. thrust / guardian
C. foremost / blotchy   D. scuttled / precisely

(b). In the INDEX the words SANTA'S DAEMONS, PENNILESS BY LETTER and BARKING BABOON are in capital letters

A. ...because they are the titles of the passages.
B. ...because they are common nouns.
C. ...because they are in the INDEX.
D. ...because they come at the end of the test.

Choose the correct noun from the list in each sentence.

60. (a) People who need legal help will first go to a
         dentist   priest   doctor   solicitor.
            A   B   C   D

(b). Research into scientific research and development usually takes place in a   factory   laboratory   canteen   workshop.
                                          A   B   C   D

GLOSSARY

bestowed------ presented, conferred, gave
bound---------- tied with string or rope
thrust---------- threw with force
sleigh---------- a vehicle without wheels for snow
noose---------- loop on a rope
glee------------ joy, happiness
foremost------- first in time, place or importance
kidnapped---- seized and held usually by force
guardian-------- person legally responsible for children
balance-------- amount that's remaining
casket--------- small box for valuables
pawning------- leaving an item as security for money borrowed
reassuring----- restoring confidence
intimidating-- threatening, frightening
scuttled------- ran with short quick steps
blotchy-------- discoloured, stained
precisely------ exactly, correctly

INDEX

NEW TRANSFER TESTS

MULTIPLE-CHOICE

ENGLISH

Practice Test 11

<u>Guidance for completing this Test.</u>

1. Read the passages carefully.

2. Read the questions thoroughly.

3. Read the answers carefully.

4. Choose what you think is the correct answer carefully.

5. Underline or circle the answer, immediately after the question.

6. Transfer the LETTER **A,B,C,D,E** or **N** to the answer sheet.

7. Make sure to mark the answer box like [—] not [/].

8. Check carefully that you have transferred your correct answer.

9 . This test lasts for **50 minutes**.

PUPIL'S NAME _____

TOTAL MARK (Out of 60)	

Read this passage and answer the questions which follow.
If there are any words you don't understand you may find
them in the Glossary at the end of the test.

MARMEE and FOUR DAUGHTERS

1.   As young readers like to know 'how people look', we will
take this moment to give them a little sketch of the four sisters,
who sat knitting away in the twilight, while the December snow
fell quietly without, and the fire crackled cheerfully within.

5.   It was a comfortable room, though the carpet was faded and the
furniture very plain, for a good picture or two hung on the walls,
books filled the recesses, chrysanthemums and Christmas roses
bloomed in the windows, and a pleasant atmosphere of home
peace pervaded it.

10.   Margaret, the eldest of the four, was sixteen, and very pretty,
being plump and fair, with large eyes, plenty of soft brown hair, a
sweet mouth, and white hands, of which she was rather vain.
Fifteen-year-old Jo was very tall, thin, and brown, and reminded
one of a colt, for she never seemed to know what to do with her

15.   long limbs, which were very much in her way. She had a decided
mouth, a comical nose, and sharp, grey eyes, which appeared to
see everything, and were by turns fierce, funny, or thoughtful.
    Her long, thick hair was her one beauty, but it was usually
bundled into a net, to be out of her way. Round shoulders had Jo,

20.   big hands and feet, a flyaway look to her clothes, and the
uncomfortable appearance of a girl who was rapidly shooting up
into a woman and didn't like it. Elizabeth, or Beth, as everyone
called her, was a rosy, smooth-haired, bright-eyed girl of thirteen,
with a shy manner, a timid voice, and a peaceful expression which

25.   was seldom disturbed.
    Her father called her 'Little Miss Tranquility', and the name
suited her excellently, for she seemed to live in a happy world of
her own, only venturing out to meet the few whom she trusted and
loved. Amy, though the youngest, was a most important person, in

30.   her own opinion at least. A regular snow maiden, with blue eyes,
and yellow hair curling on her shoulders, pale and slender, and
always carrying herself like a young lady mindful of her manners.
What the characters of the four sisters were we will leave to be
found out.

35.   The clock struck six and, having swept up the hearth, Beth
put a pair of slippers down to warm. Somehow the sight of the old
shoes had a good effect upon the girls, for Mother was coming,
and everyone brightened to welcome her. Meg stopped lecturing,

1.

40. and lighted the lamp, Amy got out of the easy chair without being asked, and Jo forgot how tired she was as she sat up to hold the slippers nearer to the blaze.

"They are quite worn out. Marmee must have a new pair."

"I thought I'd get her some with my dollar," said Beth.

"No, I shall!" cried Amy.

45. "I'm the oldest," began Meg, but Jo cut in with a decided, "I'm the man of the family now Papa is away, and I shall provide the slippers, for he told me to take special care of Mother while he was gone."

Answer the following questions. Look back over the passage. You should choose the _best_ answer and mark its letter on your answer sheet.

1. The first who suggested buying Mother a new pair of slippers was

A. Marmee   B. Beth   C. Jo   D. Amy   E. Meg

2. At the beginning of the story the four sisters were

A. ...lighting the fire.   B. ...reading their novels.
C. ...getting the dinner ready.   D. ...knitting.
E. ...listening to a lecture.

3. What other name was used for Beth ?

A. Marmee   B. Meg   C. Elizabeth
D. Margaret   E. Jo

4. What other name was used for Margaret ?

A. Marmee   B. Meg   C. Elizabeth
D. Beth   E. Jo

5. At what time did Mother come down to the sisters ?

A. ...at midnight.   B. ...at midday.
C. ...at 6 o'clock in the evening.   D. ...at 11 o'clock.
E. ...at 6 o'clock in the morning.

2.

6.   The description used for Amy is

A.   ...youngest, blue eyes, yellow hair.
B.   ...youngest, bright eyes, smooth hair.
C.   ...oldest, blue eyes, yellow hair.
D.   ...oldest, bright eyes, smooth hair.
E.   ...youngest, timid voice, shy.

7.   Beth had the quietest personality of the four sisters because

A.   ...she had smooth hair.
B.   ...she had a peaceful expression.
C.   ...she was rather vain.
D.   ...she had a timid voice.
E.   ...she had yellow hair.

8.   How do we know from the first paragraph that the sisters lived
     in an ordinary house that had simple contents ?

A.   ...roses and chrysanthemums were growing.
B.   ...there were windows.
C.   ...it had a faded carpet and plain furniture.
D.   ...books filled the recesses.
E.   ...there was a fire burning.

9.   Which of the sisters was nick-named **'Little Miss Tranquility'** ?

A.   Beth   B.   Amy
C.   Margaret   D.   Jo
E.   Meg

10. **'Little Miss Tranquility'** was named as such by her father because

A.   ...she was a bright-eyed thirteen-year-old.
B.   ...she had smooth hair and a rosy complexion.
C.   ...was tall and thin with long limbs like a colt.
D.   ...she had a sweet mouth and white hands.
E.   ...she seemed to live in a happy world of her own.

The following passage contains a number of mistakes. You have to find the mistakes. On each line there is either _one_ mistake or _no_ mistake. Find the group of words in which there is a mistake and mark the letter for it on your answer sheet. If there is no mistake, mark N.

First, look for the _spelling_ mistakes.

11. Everyone thought | soberly for | a minite, | then Meg
        A   B   C   D   N

12. anounced, as | if the idea | was suggested | by the sight of
        A   B   C   D   N

13. her own | pretty hands, | "I shall give her | a nice pear of gloves."
        A   B   C   D   N

14. "Some hankerchiefs, | all coloured, | all hemmed," | said Beth.
        A   B   C   D   N

15. "I'll get a | little bottle of | cologne. She likes | it, and it
        A   B   C   D   N

16. won't cost much, | so I'll have | sum left to | buy my pencils,"
        A   B   C   D   N

17. added Amy. | "How will we | give the things?" | asked Meg.
        A   B   C   D   N

18. "Put them on | the tabel, and | bring her in | and see her
        A   B   C   D   N

19. open the bundles. | Don't you | remembar how | we used to
        A   B   C   D   N

do it on our birthdays?" answered Jo.

20. "I used to be | so frightenned | when it was | my turn to sit
        A   B   C   D   N

Now look for _punctuation_ mistakes.

21. in the chair | with the Crown on | and see you | all come
        A   B   C   D   N

22. marching round | to g'ive the | presents, with | a kiss. I liked
        A   B   C   D   N

4.

23.	the things and	the kisses	but it was	dreadful to have
A	B	C	D	N

24.	you sit	looking at me	while I opened	the bundles ?"
A	B	C	D	N

25.	said beth, who	was toasting	her face and	the bread for
A	B	C	D	N

tea at the same time.

26.	"Let Marmee	think we are	getting things	for ourselves,
A	B	C	D	N

27.	and then	surprise her.	we must go	shopping tomorrow
A	B	C	D	N

28.	afternoon, Meg ,	There is so	much to do	about the play
A	B	C	D	N

for Christmas night," said Jo.

Read this passage and answer the questions which follow. If there are any words you don't understand you may find them in the Glossary at the end of the test.

BOOK REVIEW

1.   **Five on a Treasure Island**, published in 1942 is a popular children's book written by Enid Blyton. It is the first book in The Famous Five series. The first edition of the book was illustrated by Eileen Soper.

5.   **Plot Summary**
      Twelve year old Julian, his eleven year old brother Dick and ten year old sister Anne are chatting with their parents around the breakfast table about the family's summer holiday plans. The three children usually accompany their parents to the resort of Polseath,
10. but this year will be different as their parents intend to travel alone to Scotland instead.
      The three children will take their first holiday alone and stay with their Aunt Fanny and Uncle Quentin in the seaside town of Kirrin. The children are excited about the holiday, particularly as
15. they will meet their cousin Georgina for the first time. Georgina, they are told, is the same age as Dick, and an only child.

The children are driven down to Kirrin where they meet their kindly Aunt Fanny and her short-tempered husband, Quentin. Uncle Quentin is a brilliant scientist, who spends most of his time
20.   holed up in his study working on his experiments. Quentin does not earn enough money to keep his family properly—Georgina does not attend boarding school like her cousins, and the household does not have a hired cook or domestic staff.

Georgina turns out to be rather different from the demure
25.   little girl her cousins were expecting. The eleven year old girl wants to be a boy, cuts her hair short, wears boy's clothing and refuses to answer to her given name of Georgina, instructing her cousins to call her George instead. She is very reluctant to be friendly with her three cousins and does not make them feel
30.   welcome in her home.

Julian explains that he and the two others are willing to be friendly, but they will not beg George to be their friend. George begins to warm to them after they explain this to her. George, it turns out, is keeping a dog in secret from her father, who has
35.   forbidden her to have one.

The dog, a large mongrel named Timothy, is being kept by a local fisherman, for which she pays all her pocket money. Julian, Dick and Anne agree to keep Timothy a secret. George promises to take them to visit the little island in the bay, which she claims is
40.   hers, a gift from her mother who owned the land.

The children row over to the island and visit the wreck of a ship which is submerged just below the rocks. The ship was carrying gold, George explains, but the treasure was never found even though divers searched the ship thoroughly. That very night,
45.   there is a huge storm which lifts the wreck up onto the rocks. The children are very excited and decide to row out to the wreck and explore it, thinking that they might be able to find the gold missed by the divers. The children find only a wooden box lined with tin.

29.   Who created the illustrations in Enid Blyton's book, **"Five on a Treasure Island"** ?

A.   Enid Blyton   B.   Uncle Quentin
C.   Aunt Fanny   D.   Georgina
E.   Eileen Soper

30.   Who is the same age as Dick ?

A.   Julian   B.   Georgina   C.   Timothy
D.   Quentin   E.   Anne

6.

31. While on holiday the children will stay

A.   in Kirrin   B.   in Polseath   C.   in a hotel
D.   on an island   E.   on a ship

32. What did the children find on the wreck of the ship ?

A.   gold coins   B.   tin
C.   wooden box   D.   gold jewellery
E.   wooden box lined with tin

33. Georgina is different from her cousins because

A.   ...she goes to boarding school.
B.   ...she is the same age as Dick.
C.   ...she doesn't go to boarding school.
D.   ...she is older than any of them.
E.   ...she is younger than any of them.

34. Georgina told her cousins that

A.   ...her uncle owned the island.
B.   ...her father allows her to have a dog.
C.   ...she doesn't get any pocket money.
D.   ...she owns the island.
E.   ...she owns a small poodle dog.

35. What is unusual about the holiday of the three children ?

A.   ...the whole family was to go together to Spain.
B.   ...the three children were going on their own for the second time.
C.   ...their parents would meet up with them in a week's time.
D.   ...the children were taking a dog with them.
E.   ...they were to stay at a holiday resort.

36. Uncle Quentin is

A.   a teacher.   B.   studying to be a scientist.
C.   a doctor.   D.   working on a secret project.
E.   a brilliant scientist.

7.

37. The two reasons that tell us that Georgina wants to be a boy are

A.   ...she is eleven years old and lives with her parents.
B.   ...she has a dog and owns an island.
C.   ...she cuts her hair short and wants to be called George.
D.   ...she doesn't like her cousins and she's an only child.
E.   ...her father is a scientist and she doesn't attend boarding school.

38. How did the wreck of the ship finish up on the rocks ?

A.   ...a huge storm lifted the ship from just below the rocks.
B.   ...a big crane lifted it using steel ropes.
C.   ...the waves washed it on to the rocks.
D.   ...local fisherman tied ropes to it and lifted it.
E.   ...the wreck floated up on to the rocks.

39. The four **pronouns** in lines **17, 18 and 19** are

A.   who, are, where, down   B.   driven, meet, is, spends
C.   Kirrin, Aunt, Quentin, Fanny   D.   his, her, they, their
E.   a, of, to, the

40. The word in **lines 41 and 42** which means
    "gone below the surface" is

A.   island   B.   rocks   C.   submerged
D.   wreck   E.   ship

41. The punctuations in **line 44** are

A.   comma / question mark   B.   full stop / apostrophe
C.   question mark / full stop   D.   comma / full stop
E.   exclamation mark / comma

42. The word in **line 3** which means **"provided pictures"** is

A.   Famous   B.   series   C.   edition
D.   book   E.   illustrated

8.

Read this passage and answer the questions which follow. If there are any words you don't understand you may find them in the Glossary at the end of the test.

TENTING IN THE OPEN

1.   There can be few things that gladden the heart on an early Summer morning more than getting the tent out of the attic and heading out into the countryside. The thought of a night under the stars, the comforting rustle of a night breeze on the fly-sheet, the
5.   scuffle of early morning rabbits playing around the guy ropes; there's just nothing like camping for getting away from it all and getting back to nature.

       Sadly, the dream and the reality, as anyone who has ever stayed at a campsite knows, are often poles apart. Even at so-called
10. quiet sites "getting away from it all" seldom includes escaping the loud brash arguments of nearby tent dwellers and their hyperactive children, or, worse still, the high decibels spewing from the satellite-assisted televisions in campervans.

Furthermore, go to one of the ever-increasing crop of super-sized
15. sites and the closest you are likely to get to anything natural is losing your footing near the sluice for the chemical toilets.
Roughly 20,000 Britons can be found under canvas on any given night from May to September but it's no surprise that many are turning their backs on organised sites and going camping in the
20. open countryside, commonly called "wild camping".

       Given the unregulated nature of the activity the full extent of the pastime's popularity can only be guessed at. However, there are a lot of tenters out there in remote spots, erecting tents, cooking in the outdoors, enjoying the fresh air and of course the regular rainy
25. periods and digging little holes in the ground for toilet purposes.

       The practice of plopping one's tent down in a field or on some mountainside without paying anyone for the privilege might once have been the preserve of people with a dedicated love of the outdoors but wild camping is inching its way into the mainstream
30. as campsiters wake up to the fact that these pioneers might actually be on to something.

       A wild camping trip makes for a pretty eco-friendly break (provided you leave the car at home) while offering a good deal more in the way of adventure than a cheap return flight to Bulgaria.
35. Furthermore, it's the ultimate in budget holidays; once you've got to wherever you're going, the only expense is feeding yourself.

       Of greater value than the views and the vital food though, is the sense of freedom that simply cannot be derived from a night at a campsite, no matter how laid back the owner. Whereas campsiting

40. is the outdoors equivalent of spending a night at a hotel to which you just happen to have brought your own bed, wild camping gives you a genuine feel of the countryside, not once removed from it. Coupled with this is the excitement that comes with making yourself slightly vulnerable: out in the wild, there's no one
45. watching over you and, in really remote places, just as in outer space, no one can hear you scream.

43. In the **last paragraph** the outdoor equivalent of spending a night in an hotel is

A   ...wild camping.   B.   ...campsiting.
C.   ...outer space.   D.   ...vital food.
E.   ...bringing your own bed.

44. The loud noise coming from satellite-assisted TVs can be heard

A.   ...in the countryside   B.   ...in the hotel
C.   ...in a campsite   D.   ...one's own tent
E.   ...in remote spots

45. People who like **"getting away from it all"** want to escape from

A.   ...city life   B.   ...the loud brash arguments
C.   ...the countryside   D.   ...the chemical toilets
E.   ...Bulgaria

46. Besides **really remote places** no one can hear you scream

A.   ...in the bathroom   B.   ...in a tent
C.   ...in outer space   D.   ...in an aeroplane
E.   ...in you own bed

47. The noises that are mentioned in the **first paragraph** are

A.   ...breeze and night   B.   ...rustle and scuffle
C.   ...fly-sheet and nature   D.   ...stars and rabbits
E.   ...camping and thought

48. The usual tenting season is

A. ...all the year round
B. ...from January to June
C. ...from June to December
D. ...from May to September
E. ...in July and August

49. What helps to make a tenting break more eco-friendly ?

A. ...taking the car
B. ...reusing your washing water
C. ...taking a gas stove
D. ...leaving the car at home
E. ...travelling alone

50. Once you've arrived at your destination wild camping is **"the ultimate in budget holidays" (line 35)** because

A. ...you don't have to pay for accommodation.
B. ...you don't have any parking charges.
C. ...you have your own bed with you.
D. ...you have your flights already paid.
E. ...you have only to pay for your food.

51. Approximately how many people from Britain camp outside on any given night from May to September ?

A. 2,000
B. 10,000
C. 100,000
D. 20,000
E. 5,000

52. The word in **lines 28 to 30**, which can be used to describe people **"with a dedicated love of the outdoors" (lines 28 and 29)** is

A. campsiters
B. pioneers
C. actually
D. preserve
E. mainstream

53. In the **last paragraph** the Past tense is used in the words

A. campsiting / sense
B. making / spending
C. camping / excitement
D. brought / derived
E. slightly / simply

11.

54. The **TWO** adjectives in **line 21** are

A. given / extent
B. unregulated / full
C. nature / activity
D. nature / given
E. full / extent

55. The word in **line 44** which means **defenceless** or **exposed to danger** is

A. vulnerable
B. slightly
C. wild
D. there's
E. yourself

General Section

To answer these questions, you may have to think about the passages you have read. Look back at these if you need to. Look also at the Index and Glossary.

56. (a)   The correct pair of **plurals** is

A. echos / shelfs
B. lorries / monkeys
C. dozen / sheeps
D. man-of-wars / oxen

(b).   The correct pair of **past tenses** is

A. singed / spoke
B. awaked / falled
C. beated / freezed
D. awoke / flew

57. (a) A book which contains lots of rhyming words and verses is a

A. ...book of prose
B. ...book of poetry
C. ...book of essays
D. ...book of homonymns

(b).   The part of this test in which the main emphasis is on the outdoor life is

A. MARMEE and the FOUR DAUGHTERS
B. BOOK REVIEW
C. TENTING IN THE OPEN
D. General Section

58. (a)   The sentence which is **grammatically incorrect** is

A.   He has forgot his address.
B.   John and I played football together.
C.   This end of the rope is the thicker.
D.   One of the three boys was playing the piano.

(b).   **Apostrophes** are punctuation marks used

A.   ...to show when there is direct speech.
B.   ...to show when there is a pause in a sentence.
C.   ...to show possession or for abbreviations.
D.   ...to show that a question has been asked.

59. (a)   The **incorrect** collective phrase is

A.   ...an army of sailors   B.   ...a choir of singers
C.   ...a troop of monkeys   D.   ...a school of whales

Choose the correct word from the list in each sentence.

(b).   The girls say that   **there**   **their**   **they're**   **theire**   going
                              A   B   C   D
on holiday next week.

60. (a)   Last week the pupils   **going**   **gone**   **went**   **arrived**   to
                                   A   B   C   D
the swimming pool for a gala.

(b).   The word which has a **different meaning** than the other
       three in the group is

A.   accurate   B.   mark
C.   exact   D.   correct

GLOSSARY

recesses------------ gaps, openings between furniture
limbs--------------- arms and legs
colt---------------- young male horse
edition------------- copy of a new publication
illustrated--------- explanation using pictures, drawings
accompany-------- to go along with
domestic----------- belonging to a house or family
demure------------- quiet, shy, reserved
reluctant----------- unwilling
mongrel------------ dog of mixed breed
hyperactive------- excessively active
decibels----------- measurement of noise level
spewing----------- sending out in a stream
unregulated------- without rules or regulation
privilege----------- advantage or favour
vulnerable--------- liable to get hurt
remote------------- far away, distant

INDEX

NEW TRANSFER TESTS

MULTIPLE-CHOICE
ENGLISH
Practice Test 12

Guidance for completing this Test.

1.   Read the passages carefully.

2.   Read the questions thoroughly.

3.   Read the answers carefully.

4.   Choose what you think is the correct answer carefully.

5.   Underline or circle the answer, immediately after the
      question.

6.   Transfer the LETTER **A,B,C,D,E** or **N** to the answer sheet.

7.   Make sure to mark the answer box like [—] not [/].

8.   Check carefully that you have transferred your correct answer.

9 .   This test lasts for **50 minutes.**

PUPIL'S NAME _____

TOTAL MARK (Out of 60)	

Read this passage and answer the questions which follow. If there are any words you don't understand you may find them in the Glossary at the end of the test.

MARIE CURIE BIOGRAPHY

1.   Marie Sklodovska was the youngest of 5 children, born in 1867, Warsaw, Poland. She was brought up in a poor but well educated family. Marie excelled in her studies and won many prizes. At an early age she became committed to the ideal of Polish
5.   independence from Russia which was currently ruling Poland with an iron fist, and in particular making life difficult for intellectuals.

      She yearned to be able to teach fellow Polish women who were mostly condemned to zero education. Unusually for women at that
10.   time, Marie took an interest in Chemistry and Biology. Since opportunities in Poland for further study were limited, Marie went to Paris, where, after working as a governess, she was able to study at the Sorbonne, Paris. She struggled to learn in French but went on to get a degree in Physics finishing top in her school. She later
15.   got a degree in Maths, finishing second in her school year.

      It was in Paris, that she met Pierre Curie, who was then chief of the laboratory at the school of Physics and Chemistry. He was a renowned chemist, who had conducted many experiments on crystals and electronics. Pierre and Marie were married in Paris in
20.   July 1895.

      Marie pursued studies in radioactivity. In 1898, this led to the discovery of two new elements, one of which she named polonium after her home country. There then followed 4 years of extensive study into the properties of radium. Using dumped uranium
25.   tailings from a nearby mine, they were very slowly, and painstakingly, able to extract a decigram of radium.

      Radium was discovered to have remarkable impacts. Marie actually suffered burns from the rays. It was from this discovery of radium and its properties that the science of radiation was able to
30.   develop, using the properties of radium to burn away diseased cells in the body.

      The Curies agreed to give away their secret freely; they did not wish to patent such a valuable element. The element was soon in high demand and it began industrial scale production.
35.   For their discovery they were awarded the Davy Medal, a British award and the renowned Nobel Prize for physics in 1903.

      In 1905, Pierre was killed in a road accident, leaving Marie to look after the laboratory and her two children. In 1911 she was

40. awarded a second nobel prize in Chemistry for the discovery of actinium and further studies on radium and polonium. The success of Marie Curie also brought considerable hostility, criticism and suspicion from a male dominated science world.

The onset of World War I in 1914, led to Marie Curie dedicating her time to the installation of X ray machines in
45. hospitals. By the end of the first world war, over a million soldiers had been examined by her X ray units.

Marie Curie died in 1934 from cancer. It was an unfortunate side effect of her own groundbreaking studies into radiation which were to help so many people. Marie Curie pushed back many
50. frontiers in science; and at the same time set a new bar for female academic and scientific achievement. One of the largest Cancer charities in the United Kingdom is named after Marie Curie.

Answer the following questions. Look back over the passage. You should choose the _best_ answer and mark its letter on your answer sheet.

1. In what **year** was Marie's husband Pierre killed ?

A. 1934   B. 1914   C. 1911
D. 1905   E. 1903

2. Apart from herself **how many** other children were there in the Sklodovska family ?

A. 6   B. 5   C. 4
D. 3   E. 2

3. Marie Curie won the Nobel prize in 1911 for

A. ...her discovery of radium.
B. ...her discovery of X rays.
C. ...her discovery of polonium.
D. ...her discovery of actinium.
E. ...her discovery of radiation.

4. What made Marie Curie dedicate her work to installing X ray machines in hospitals ?

A. ...the death of her husband in an accident.
B. ...her work was being criticised by other male scientists.
C. ...her winning of the Davy Medal.
D. ...radium was produced on an industrial scale.
E. ...the beginning of World War 1 in 1914.

2.

5. From an early age Marie Curie was committed to

A. ...emigrating from her native Poland.
B. ...the ideal of Polish independence from Russia.
C. ...staying in Poland as a politician.
D. ...carrying on her studies in the United Kingdom.
E. ...making sure the poor were helped out of poverty.

6. What enabled Marie Curie to study in Paris ?

A. ...her father gave her a scholarship.
B. ...she worked in Paris as a governess.
C. ...the university gave her a bursary.
D. ...she had taught women in Poland.
E. ...she had an interest in Chemistry and Biology.

7. Marie Curie met her husband Pierre when he

A. ...was working as a teacher in Warsaw, Marie's home city.
B. ...had travelled to Poland for a job interview.
C. ...was the laboratory chief in the Paris university.
D. ...visited her when she was a graduate in Paris.
E. ...discovered the elements radium, polonium and actinium.

8. Why was radium such an important discovery ?

A. ...it was cheaper than the existing drugs.
B. ...it replaced the uranium that had been used before.
C. ...its properties were able to burn away diseased body cells.
D. ...it was easy to extract from uranium.
E. ...it made Marie and her husband very famous.

9. Russia, who ruled Poland, made life difficult for

A. scientists   B. Polish people
C. intellectuals   D. teachers
E. Russian people

10. The amount of radium first extracted by Marie from uranium was

A. 1 kilogram   B. 1 ounce   C. 1 millilitre
D. 1 decigram   E. 1 milligram

3.

The following passage contains a number of mistakes. You have to find the mistakes. On each line there is either _one_ mistake or _no_ mistake. Find the group of words in which there is a mistake and mark the letter for it on your answer sheet. If there is no mistake, mark N.

First, look for the _spelling_ mistakes.

11. | While employen | more than | 2,700 nurses, | doctors and other | |
| :-: | :-: | :-: | :-: | :-: |
| A | B | C | D | N |

12. | healthcare | profesionals, | we expect to | provide care to | |
| :-: | :-: | :-: | :-: | :-: |
| A | B | C | D | N |

13. | around 25,000 | terminally ill | patients in | the comunity | |
| :-: | :-: | :-: | :-: | :-: |
| A | B | C | D | N |

14. | and in our | hospices this year, | along with | support for there | |
| :-: | :-: | :-: | :-: | :-: |
| A | B | C | D | N |

15. | families. We | manely care | for people with | cancer but we | |
| :-: | :-: | :-: | :-: | :-: |
| A | B | C | D | N |

16. | also care for people | with other | life limiting | illneses. Our | |
| :-: | :-: | :-: | :-: | :-: |
| A | B | C | D | N |

17. | services are | always free of | charge to patients | and their | |
| :-: | :-: | :-: | :-: | :-: |
| A | B | C | D | N |

18. | familys. The | charity is best | known for its | network of Marie | |
| :-: | :-: | :-: | :-: | :-: |
| A | B | C | D | N |

19. | Curie Norses | working in the | community to | provide care | |
| :-: | :-: | :-: | :-: | :-: |
| A | B | C | D | N |

for patients in their own homes.

20. | We have ten | hospices across | Ingland, Scotland, | Wales and | |
| :-: | :-: | :-: | :-: | :-: |
| A | B | C | D | N |

Now look for _punctuation_ mistakes.

21. | Northern ireland, | and two centres | for research | into the | |
| :-: | :-: | :-: | :-: | :-: |
| A | B | C | D | N |

disease.

4.

22. Financially " around | seventy per cent | of the | charity's income
     A · B · C · D · N

23. comes from | the generous | support of | thousands of
     A · B · C · D · N

24. individuals, | membership, | Organisations | and businesses,
     A · B · C · D · N

25. with the | balance of our, | funds coming | from the NHS,
     A · B · C · D · N

26. We also depend | on an army | of volunteer's | to support our
     A · B · C · D · N

27. work in both | care and | fundraising. The | daffodil is the
     A · B · C · D · N

28. emblem of the | charity Every | March we run | the Daffodil
     A · B · C · D · N

Appeal, with fundraising events nationwide.

**Read this passage and answer the questions which follow.
If there are any words you don't understand you may find
them in the Glossary at the end of the test.**

BEIJING IN WINTER

1.   This is how you talk about a city you love. You talk about it
as if it's the only place in the world where this story can happen.
A friend of mine fell in love with someone when she went for a bite
at a *malatang* one winter night. There was no snow; there is very
5.   little snowfall during Beijing winters.
      The film below the skies turns from yellow to gray, then the
winds from Mongolia come and we would say, it's so cold already
there might as well be snow. Some days there are, and those are the
days when photographers go out to make postcards of fresh powder
10. collecting over the shoulders of the stone lion finials perched on
the gables of the Forbidden City.
      But those are postcards. There are times you feel cheated
when you glance at them and wonder at your inability to recall a
greater feeling of grandeur when you had bought them in front of
15. the pagoda. The event, like infinity, had been too big to be grasped
and had only given way to frustration, a voice insisting with the
strongest conviction and the vaguest meaning that there should
have been something more.

5.

20. I had flown to China with a postcard of Beijing in my hand. My grandmother didn't want me to. Why should I go back to the place she had taken so many pains to run away from sixty years ago to get to Manila? The Philippines was glamorous then, before it melted in its own laziness. Europe and America mixed in Asia, because the sun never sets in the Western empire. Before I left for the airport,
25. my grandmother told me to be careful in the mud alleys.

The postcard I had was a picture of a language university in Beijing that specialized in teaching Mandarin to foreigners. Once in the Philippines, when I was eleven, I had to recite the week's lesson from memory to the teacher in Mandarin class. This was
30. the way we learned the language carved on wooden slabs in a tiny family shrine somewhere across the ocean.

I had spent the night before reading out loud from my little exercise book and hoping school would be cancelled the next morning. It was monsoon season and the floods rose from the
35. gutters blocked with garbage and the beggars' children played naked in the waters. But the storm left at dawn, and memory is unreliable, selective, compressed. The next day I finally received on my palm the two red stripes that I had been avoiding during the entirety of my young life in school.
40. Eight years later I was sent to Beijing with my parents' blessings, and a friend of mine fell in love one winter night when she went to the *malatang*. I'm here to tell you what Beijing was like beyond the language classes. *Malatang* was a street-vendor's boiler filled with skewers of meats, innards, seaweed, tofu, and
45. mushrooms that floated in a dark oily soup of chilli and cayenne pepper.

Malatang was huddling together with strangers who looked like you and reading advertisements pasted on electric poles. *Malatang* was sucking the bitter north wind to cool the spice in
50. your mouth and keeping your eyes from tearing, while the vendor counted the wooden skewers that you had speared into your broken half of a Styrofoam rice box.

29. What was perched on the gables of the Forbidden City ?

A.   ...photographers.   B.   ...stone lion finials.
C.   ...postcards.   D.   ...yellow and gray skies.
E.   ...a malatang.

30. The Chinese city that has the name **"Forbidden City"** is :-

A.   Mongolia   B.   Manila   C.   Philippines
D.   Asia   E.   Beijing

6.

31. A street-vendor's boiler filled with food is called

A. ...an oven
C. ...Styrofoam rice box
E. ...Mandarin

B. ...wooden skewers
D. ...a malatang

32. The photographers go out to make postcards when

A. ...the stone lions shine brightly.
B. ...the skies turn from yellow to gray.
C. ...the little snow collects on the shoulders of the lion finials.
D. ...they are bought in front of the pagoda.
E. ...the winds blow in from Mongolia.

33. The author's grandmother had run away from

A. Beijing
D. Mandarin

B. Manila
E. Philippines

C. Mongolia

34. The university in Beijing specialised in

A. ...teaching pupils to recite Mandarin poetry.
B. ...teaching Chinese how to cook in a malatang.
C. ...teaching Science subjects to medical students.
D. ...nuclear physics.
E. ...teaching Mandarin to foreigners.

35. How did the author learn the Mandarin language ?

A. ...parents and grandparents.
B. ...from the language which was carved on wooden slabs.
C. ...at the university of Beijing.
D. ...from foreign visitors to Manila.
E. ...in a Manila primary school.

36. What was received on the palm of the author's hands ?

A. ...a malatang
D. ...a picture

B. ...two red stripes
E. ...a Mandarin poem

C. ...a shrine

37. The author's grandmother had left China

A. ...last year   B. ...in 1949
C. ...10 years ago   D. ...60 years ago
E. ...when she married

38. On what were the advertisements pasted ?

A. ...on electric poles
B. ...on shop windows
C. ...in newspapers
D. ...on the backs of buses
E. ...on Styrofoam boxes

39. The words **photographers**, **postcards** and **powder** as used in
line 9 are

A. Adjectives   B. Pronouns   C. Verbs
D. Nouns   E. Adverbs

40. The phrase **"inability to recall"** in **line 13** means the same as :-

A. ...memorising fluently
B. ...remembering always
C. ...talent for recollecting
D. ...unable to remember
E. ...fresh in my mind

41. The adjectives in **line 17** are :-

A. conviction and meaning
B. should and strongest
C. strongest and vaguest
D. there and that
E. vaguest and conviction

42. The words **China, America and Philippines** are the names of

A. ...villages   B. ...towns   C. ...cities
D. ...countries   E. ...continents

8.

Read this passage and answer the questions which follow. If there are any words you don't understand you may find them in the Glossary at the end of the test.

STATS ABOUT LIONS

1.   Lions eat large prey, such as gazelles, antelopes, zebras, wildebeests, and buffalo. They have been known to take down prey as large as a young giraffe. Most prey animals can run much faster than the average lion. Therefore, lions hunt in fairly well organised

5. groups and stalk, or sneak up on, their prey. They may try to surround them first, then make a swift, sudden charge from the tall grass. The grass where lions live is not short and green but grows very tall and is a light brownish color most of the time. The lions' fur is the same colour as this grass, making it difficult for other

10. animals to see them. Coloring that helps to hide an animal or thing is called "camouflage".

        Females do most of the hunting and work in groups although, if she has to, a single lioness is able to hunt on her own. Male lions are actually more capable hunters than females but they usually

15. focus more on protecting the pride. Lions might spend hours stalking prey but the actual kill is made in just minutes.

        After a kill is made, the females let out low roars. This tells the pride to join them for a meal. Adult males eat first, followed by females, and then cubs. To avoid the dangerous heat of the

20. mid-day sun, lions usually hunt at night when the dim light helps to keep them hidden from their prey. Lions have very good night vision so the darkness does not pose a problem for them. Animals that are active at night like lions are called nocturnal creatures.

FUN FACTS

25. • A male lion has a mane of long fur around his face.
     • A male lion's roar can be heard up to 5 miles away.
     • The hunting grounds for a pride of lions can range from 8 to 150 square miles.
     • The largest lion on record was almost 11 feet long and
30.   weighed nearly 700 pounds.
     • Lions rarely eat an entire kill. Hyenas and vultures finish the rest.
     • A lion can run as fast as 35 mph for short distances and can leap over objects up to 30 feet tall.
35. • The number of lions in Africa is one fourth of the number there was just 40 years ago.
     • A lion's eyesight is five times better than a human, and it can hear prey that is more than a mile away.
     • It may take up to 4 hours for a pride of lions to finish eating.

Multiple Choice English

Test 12 Answer Key.

MARIE CURIE BIOGRAPHY
1. D
2. C
3. D
4. E
5. B
6. B
7. C
8. C
9. C
10. D

Spelling
11. A--employing
12. B--professionals
13. D--community
14. D--their
15. B--mainly
16. D--illnesses
17. N
18. A--families
19. A--Nurses
20. C--England

Punctuation
21. A--Ireland
22. A--no speech marks
23. N
24. C--organisations
25. B--no full stop
26. C--no apostrophe
27. N
28. B--every

BEIJING IN WINTER
29. B
30. E
31. D
32. C
33. A
34. E
35. B
36. B
37. D
38. A
39. D
40. D
41. C
42. D

STATS ABOUT LIONS
43. C
44. C
45. A
46. A
47. B
48. E
49. B
50. D
51. C
52. E
53. C
54. B
55. D

General Section
56.	(a)	C	(b).	A
57.	(a)	D	(b).	B
58.	(a)	C	(b).	B
59.	(a)	C	(b).	D
60.	(a)	C	(b).	D

Multiple Choice English
Test 10 Answer Key.

SANTA'S DAEMONS
1. D
2. E
3. C
4. A
5. D
6. D
7. B
8. E
9. B
10. E

Punctuation
11. B--happened
12. C--sleigh
13. N
14. N
15. C--helping
16. C--their
17. D--were
18. A--tucked
19. N
20. A--knew

Punctuation
21. C--their
22. C--journeys
23. A--no exclamation mark
24. N
25. D--no question mark
26. C--no full stop
27. D--halt
28. A--Peter

PENNILESS BY LETTER
29. C
30. D
31. B
32. A
33. C
34. D
35. D
36. D
37. C
38. E
39. C
40. C
41. B
42. D

BARKING BABOON
43. E
44. B
45. C
46. E
47. B
48. C
49. D
50. A
51. C
52. E
53. A
54. D
55. E

General Section
56.	(a)	C	(b).	B
57.	(a)	C	(b).	C
58.	(a)	D	(b).	B
59.	(a)	C	(b).	A
60.	(a)	D	(b).	B

Multiple Choice English
Test 11 Answer Key.

MARMEE and FOUR DAUGHTERS
1. C
2. D
3. C
4. B
5. C
6. A
7. D
8. C
9. A
10. E

Spelling
11. C--minute
12. A--announced
13. D--pair
14. A--handkerchiefs
15. N
16. C--some
17. N
18. B--table
19. C--remember
20. B--frightened

Punctuation
21. B--crown
22. B--no apostrophe
23. N
24. D--no question mark
25. A--Beth
26. N
27. C--We
28. A--full stop missing

BOOK REVIEW
29. E
30. B
31. A
32. E
33. C
34. D
35. B
36. E
37. C
38. A
39. D
40. C
41. D
42. E

TENTING IN THE OPEN
43. B
44. C
45. B
46. C
47. B
48. D
49. D
50. E
51. D
52. B
53. D
54. B
55. A

General Section
56.	(a)	B	(b).	D
57.	(a)	B	(b).	C
58.	(a)	A	(b).	C
59.	(a)	A	(b).	C
60.	(a)	C	(b).	B

40. • A male lion eats first, even though the females actually catch the prey.
    • After eating, a thirsty lion may drink for as long as 20 minutes.
    • There can be up to 40 members in a pride with over half of them being cubs and young adults.
45. • Females will often stay with the pride their entire life, while young males are driven out.
    • A lion eats 69 kg of meat a day.

43. How many **FUN FACTS** are listed in the passage ?

A. 10   B. 12   C. 14
D. 16   E. 18

44. Which **TWO** senses give lions a big advantage over humans ?

A. ...taste and feeling.
B. ...hearing and smell.
C. ...sight and smell.
D. ...sight and hearing
E. ...taste and touch.

45. What is unusual about what happens the young male lions in a group ?

A. ...they are hunted out of the pride.
B. ...they replace the young female lions.
C. ...they become the dominant members of the pride.
D. ...they decide to leave the pride on their own.
E. ...they are looked after by the mature male lions.

46. Lions hunt in **groups** rather than as individuals because

A. most of their prey can run much faster than lions.
B. they cannot catch their prey on their own.
C. they have to show their young how to hunt.
D. they fear being killed themselves.
E. their prey would attack them as single hunters.

47. Female lions carry out most of the hunting because

A. ...male lions are not able to hunt.
B. ...the males are better at protecting the pride.
C. ...female lions are better hunters than males.
D. ...the prey are bigger than the lions.
E. ...males take too long to make a kill.

48. The largest recorded lion was

A. 500 pound in weight and 11 feet long.
B. 700 pound in weight and 15 feet long.
C. 700 kilograms in weight and 11 metres long.
D. 11 kilograms in weight and 700 metres long.
E. 11 feet long and 700 pounds in weight.

49. Lions usually hunt at night because they

A. have poor eyesight and cannot be seen easily.
B. have excellent eyesight and the dim light keeps them hidden.
C. sleep during the day and like the sun.
D. need the light from the moon and the cover of the long grass.
E. they have more speed and their senses are sharper.

50. Lions live near a plentiful supply of water because

A. they need to wash themselves after hunting.
B. they like to swim during the day.
C. they lie in the water to cool down.
D. they have to drink water for up to 20 minutes after eating.
E. water is associated with a lion's habitat.

51. The remainder of a lion kill is usually finished off by

A. giraffes and elephants
B. wildebeests and buffalo
C. hyenas and vultures
D. tigers and humans
E. gazelles and antelopes

52. Lions and many animals are more active at night.
These types of animals are called

A. nightlighters   B. nighteaters
C. daydreamers   D. moonlighters
E. nocturnal

53. The word "**camouflage**" in the **first** paragraph means the same as

A. hidden treasure   B. lost environment
C. coloured disguise   D. open habitat
E. tall coloured grass

54. Which of the following **FUN FACTS** are **True** ?

A. A lioness has long hair around its face.
B. A pride of lions has a hunting territory of up to 150 square miles.
C. Lions finish eating their prey in an hour.
D. Lions can leap over a tree which is 40 feet high.
E. Lions can run as fast as 50 mph.

55. The word in the **second paragraph** which is an **adverb** is

A. hunting   B. although   C. single
D. usually   E. minutes

General Section
To answer these questions, you may have to think about the passages you have read. Look back at these if you need to. Look also at the Index and Glossary. Choose one of the four answers and mark the correct letter on your answer sheet.

56.   The game began in a welter of excitement but it was

(a). similar of   similar at   similar to   similar after   their previous
      A   B   C   D

(b). meeting. City   had played   was played   are played   is played
                     A   B   C   D

their country neighbours on four previous occasions. The country

57. (a) team should of | could of | would have | should have won
          A   B   C   D

(b). then but since | because | despite | however of having a player
              A   B   C   D

sent off they were unable to hold on to their early lead.

58. (a) The **Proper nouns** in the part of the passage BEIJING IN
        WINTER from **line 26** to **line 31** are :-

A. The / Once   B. Beijing / This
C. Philippines / Beijing   D. Once / Philippines

(b). The word in the Glossary which has the same meaning as
     "well-known" is :-

A. committed   B. renowned
C. stalk   D. grandeur

59. (a) Which **TWO** words in the **INDEX** are names of awards that are
        given to people who have had a great achievement ?

A. Spelling and Africa   B. Pierre Curie and Sorbonne
C. Davy medal and Nobel   D. World War 1 and Mandarin

(b). The best description of a **Contraction** is :-

A. ...words which have been joined together with a conjunction.
B. ...a word which has the opposite meaning as another word.
C. ...words which have been shortened to initials.
D. ...words have been shortened into one word using an apostrophe.

60. (a) Which pair of the following are correct **plurals** ?

A. spies / leafs   B. mice / hice
C. cargoes / roofs   D. dozen / brotheres

(b). The word which has **no singular form** is

A. spoonfuls   B. pence
C. geese   D. tongs

13.

GLOSSARY

committed---- dedicated, devoted

intellectuals-- academics, educated people

renowned------ famous, celebrated

electronics---- technology dependent on electrical devices

radioactivity-- emission of radiation

radium-------- radioactive metallic substance

decigram----- one tenth of a gram

element------- component part of a substance

hostility------- unfriendly and aggressive behaviour

suspicion------ feeling of not trusting a person or thing

gables---------- triangular upper part of the end wall of a building

grandeur------ splendour, magnificence

pagoda-------- tiered tower-shaped building common in China

conviction---- strong belief, opinion or view

shrine-------- place of worship about a sacred person or place

vendor--------- seller

skewer-------- pin to hold meat together

prey----------- animal hunted and killed by other animals

stalk---------- follow or approach in a cunning manner

INDEX

English Test 11

Please mark the boxes like (—), not like (╱). Rub out mistakes thoroughly.

Pages 2 & 3.

1 (A)(B)(C)(D)(E)	6 (A)(B)(C)(D)(E)
2 (A)(B)(C)(D)(E)	7 (A)(B)(C)(D)(E)
3 (A)(B)(C)(D)(E)	8 (A)(B)(C)(D)(E)
4 (A)(B)(C)(D)(E)	9 (A)(B)(C)(D)(E)
5 (A)(B)(C)(D)(E)	10 (A)(B)(C)(D)(E)

Pages 4

Spelling

11 (A)(B)(C)(D)(N)	16 (A)(B)(C)(D)(N)
12 (A)(B)(C)(D)(N)	17 (A)(B)(C)(D)(N)
13 (A)(B)(C)(D)(N)	18 (A)(B)(C)(D)(N)
14 (A)(B)(C)(D)(N)	19 (A)(B)(C)(D)(N)
15 (A)(B)(C)(D)(N)	20 (A)(B)(C)(D)(N)

Page 4 & 5

Punctuation

21 (A)(B)(C)(D)(N)	25 (A)(B)(C)(D)(N)
22 (A)(B)(C)(D)(N)	26 (A)(B)(C)(D)(N)
23 (A)(B)(C)(D)(N)	27 (A)(B)(C)(D)(N)
24 (A)(B)(C)(D)(N)	28 (A)(B)(C)(D)(N)

Pages 6, 7 & 8.

29 (A)(B)(C)(D)(E)	36 (A)(B)(C)(D)(E)
30 (A)(B)(C)(D)(E)	37 (A)(B)(C)(D)(E)
31 (A)(B)(C)(D)(E)	38 (A)(B)(C)(D)(E)
32 (A)(B)(C)(D)(E)	39 (A)(B)(C)(D)(E)
33 (A)(B)(C)(D)(E)	40 (A)(B)(C)(D)(E)
34 (A)(B)(C)(D)(E)	41 (A)(B)(C)(D)(E)
35 (A)(B)(C)(D)(E)	42 (A)(B)(C)(D)(E)

Pages 10, 11 & 12.

43 (A)(B)(C)(D)(E)	49 (A)(B)(C)(D)(E)
44 (A)(B)(C)(D)(E)	50 (A)(B)(C)(D)(E)
45 (A)(B)(C)(D)(E)	51 (A)(B)(C)(D)(E)
46 (A)(B)(C)(D)(E)	52 (A)(B)(C)(D)(E)
47 (A)(B)(C)(D)(E)	53 (A)(B)(C)(D)(E)
48 (A)(B)(C)(D)(E)	54 (A)(B)(C)(D)(E)
	55 (A)(B)(C)(D)(E)

Pages 12 & 13

General Section

56 (a) (A)(B)(C)(D)	58 (b) (A)(B)(C)(D)
(b) (A)(B)(C)(D)	59 (a) (A)(B)(C)(D)
57 (a) (A)(B)(C)(D)	(b) (A)(B)(C)(D)
(b) (A)(B)(C)(D)	60 (a) (A)(B)(C)(D)
58 (a) (A)(B)(C)(D)	(b) (A)(B)(C)(D)

English Test 12

Please mark the boxes like (—), not like (/). Rub out mistakes thoroughly.

Pages 2 & 3.

1	(A) (B) (C) (D) (E)	6	(A) (B) (C) (D) (E)
2	(A) (B) (C) (D) (E)	7	(A) (B) (C) (D) (E)
3	(A) (B) (C) (D) (E)	8	(A) (B) (C) (D) (E)
4	(A) (B) (C) (D) (E)	9	(A) (B) (C) (D) (E)
5	(A) (B) (C) (D) (E)	10	(A) (B) (C) (D) (E)

Pages 4

Spelling

11	(A) (B) (C) (D) (N)	16	(A) (B) (C) (D) (N)
12	(A) (B) (C) (D) (N)	17	(A) (B) (C) (D) (N)
13	(A) (B) (C) (D) (N)	18	(A) (B) (C) (D) (N)
14	(A) (B) (C) (D) (N)	19	(A) (B) (C) (D) (N)
15	(A) (B) (C) (D) (N)	20	(A) (B) (C) (D) (N)

Page 4 & 5

Punctuation

21	(A) (B) (C) (D) (N)	25	(A) (B) (C) (D) (N)
22	(A) (B) (C) (D) (N)	26	(A) (B) (C) (D) (N)
23	(A) (B) (C) (D) (N)	27	(A) (B) (C) (D) (N)
24	(A) (B) (C) (D) (N)	28	(A) (B) (C) (D) (N)

Pages 6, 7 & 8.

29	(A) (B) (C) (D) (E)	36	(A) (B) (C) (D) (E)
30	(A) (B) (C) (D) (E)	37	(A) (B) (C) (D) (E)
31	(A) (B) (C) (D) (E)	38	(A) (B) (C) (D) (E)
32	(A) (B) (C) (D) (E)	39	(A) (B) (C) (D) (E)
33	(A) (B) (C) (D) (E)	40	(A) (B) (C) (D) (E)
34	(A) (B) (C) (D) (E)	41	(A) (B) (C) (D) (E)
35	(A) (B) (C) (D) (E)	42	(A) (B) (C) (D) (E)

Pages 10, 11 & 12.

43	(A) (B) (C) (D) (E)	49	(A) (B) (C) (D) (E)
44	(A) (B) (C) (D) (E)	50	(A) (B) (C) (D) (E)
45	(A) (B) (C) (D) (E)	51	(A) (B) (C) (D) (E)
46	(A) (B) (C) (D) (E)	52	(A) (B) (C) (D) (E)
47	(A) (B) (C) (D) (E)	53	(A) (B) (C) (D) (E)
48	(A) (B) (C) (D) (E)	54	(A) (B) (C) (D) (E)
		55	(A) (B) (C) (D) (E)

Pages 12 & 13

General Section

56	(a) (A) (B) (C) (D)	58	(b) (A) (B) (C) (D)
	(b) (A) (B) (C) (D)	59	(a) (A) (B) (C) (D)
57	(a) (A) (B) (C) (D)		(b) (A) (B) (C) (D)
	(b) (A) (B) (C) (D)	60	(a) (A) (B) (C) (D)
58	(a) (A) (B) (C) (D)		(b) (A) (B) (C) (D)

Instructions for completing the Answer Sheet.

1. You must concentrate fully when recording your answers.

   --take your time when recording your answers--

   --make sure you have the correct answer number--

   --make sure you select the correct letter, A, B, C, D, E or N--

2. Use a pencil to mark your answer, A, B, C, D, E or N.

3. Mark your answer like this---- (A) (B) (C) (D) (E) (N)

   (A) (B) (C) (D) (E) (N)

   (A) (B) (C) (D) (E) (N)

   ALWAYS USE A HORIZONTAL (—) LINE

4. DO NOT MARK like this-- (A) (B) (C) (D) (E) (N)

   (A) (B) (C) (D) (E) (N)

   (A) (B) (C) (D) (E) (N)

   (A) (B) (C) (D) (E) (N)

5. If you make a mistake, rub out the line, select the correct answer and draw a line through the correct letter.

6. It might be an idea to answer 5 questions at a time and then record these 5 answers all at the same time.

7. When reading the questions you record the answers on the question paper. When you have completed 5 questions on the question paper you then record these on the Answer sheet. Proceed to record another 5 questions.